P9-DMR-416

Miss Lasko-Gross

22 Comics New York

Z2 Comics
Publisher: Josh Frankel

First Edition January 2015

ISBN-13: 978-194087027

Z2 Comics 527 Madison Ave New York, New York 10022

z2comics.com

Printed in Canada

Dedicated to Jacqui and Tod,
the most loving and supportive parents you could hope for.

DAD!
LOOK AT ME!
DAD! **DAD!**

ALL RIGHT **HENNI,** LET'S GO HOME.

YOU TOLD MOM WE WERE GOING TO TEMPLE.
YES.

WHY DID YOU LIE?

YOUR MOTHER CANNOT BE TRUSTED.

DON'T YOU LOVE HER?

...NO.

BUT YOU DO LOVE *ME*...
...DON'T YOU?

OF COURSE I DO.
DON'T BE STUPID.

HOLD HIS HEAD!

TERADICE WILL RISE, AND YOU WILL BE CRUSHED LIKE INSECTS!

A MAN WHO WON'T HEAR GOD'S TRUTH NEEDS NO EARS.

AAARR

RRRRHHHH!!

DADDY!
DON'T YOU DARE CRY.

HE BROUGHT THIS ON **HIMSELF.**
MA GA BA

TAKE YOUR **SISTER** OUT FOR A WALK.

HENNI
BY MISS LASKO-GROSS

RETURN HOME
RETURN HOME
RETURN HOME
RETURN HOME

YOU MUST BE **SO** EXCITED, HENNI.
SURE. BUT WHAT IF I HATE THE **GROOM** WHO'S CHOSEN?

IMPOSSIBLE.
THE TEMPLEMEN RECEIVE DIVINE GUIDANCE.

THE MATCH WAS WRITTEN AMONG THE STARS, LONG BEFORE YOUR BIRTH...

...SO IT CAN ONLY BE PERFECTION.
RIGHT?
YEAH...

...I GUESS.

HELLO HENNI, HELLO HILDE.
HELLO MOTHER.

OOOOH MEAT PIE!

MY FAVORITE!

SMACK!

STUPID STUPID GIRL!
GO BEG FORGIVENESS.
BUT I JUST--

DON'T ADD DISOBEDIENCE TO YOUR TRANSGRESSIONS.

NOW HENNI, THIS IS A VERY SPECIAL PIE FOR THE TEMPLEMEN.

TAKE IT TO THEM
RIGHT AWAY.
DO NOT STOP--

AND DON'T LET IT
OUT OF YOUR SIGHT--
--EVEN FOR
AN INSTANT--

DO YOU
UNDERSTAND?

YES
MOTHER.

WOW! THIS IS HEAVY PIE!

HI HENNI.
HI KORA.

ISN'T YOUR SISTER A SEASON YOUNG FOR MARRIAGE?

I'M JUST HELPING CARRY.

YEAH, THIS CAKE IS HEAVIER THAN GOD'S PEBBLE.
KORA!
A LADY DOESN'T BLASPHEME!

I WON'T EVEN BE A LADY 'TIL TOMORROW.

OH, VERY MATURE.
MOVE IT ALONG GIRLS.

A HUMBLE OFFERING...

LEAVE YOUR **HAND PRINT** UPON THE BANNER.

ACTUALLY...

FATHER TAUGHT ME TO **INSCRIBE...**
Henni

TSK-- WASTING EDUCATION ON A GIRL...
INDICATIVE OF THE LACK IN JUDGEMENT THAT DESTROYED HIM.
Henni Hoge

I'VE HEARD THIS ONE IS TROUBLE, ALWAYS WITH QUESTIONS AND OPINIONS.
A POISONED MIND. HER FATHER'S DAUGHTER.

KORA?

EVER WONDER WHY THE TEMPLE NEEDS ARMED GUARDS?

NOT REALLY.

BUT AREN'T YOU AT ALL CURIOUS?

"THE MOUSE WHO PEEKS IN THE VIPER PIT IS EATEN"

YES.
PEOPLE OFTEN QUOTE ME THAT PROVERB.

SERIOUSLY HENNI, "QUIET OBEDIENCE IS THE VERY SOURCE OF OUR UNITY."
BUT ARE WE TRULY HARMONIOUS...?

...OR SIMPLY SKILLED IN CRUSHING DISSENT?

THE RESULT IS THE SAME, SO REALLY, WHAT'S THE DIFFERENCE?

WELL, I WANT MY LOVE AND MY FAITH TO BE TRUE--
NOT JUST IDEAS RESTING ON OTHER ANCIENT, UNPROVABLE IDEAS.

YOU'RE ALWAYS SO FUNNY. I HOPE OUR HUSBANDS ALLOW US TO REMAIN FRIENDS!

WELL, I'M OFF TO GROOM FOR THE **WEDDING FESTIVAL.**

YEAH, SEE YOU **TOMORROW.**

THIS SEASON EVERYONE WANTS THE BUTCHER'S SON FOR A GROOM.

YES, BUT THE KOSTERS WANT IT A LITTLE MORE THAN THE REST.

YOU'RE LATE. TELL ME YOU DIDN'T LOSE THE PIE!

RELAX MOTHER. I DELIVERED THE **BRIBE.**

GOOD.

GOOD?
GOOD?!

≠SIGH≠ OH, MY DIFFICULT CHILD, WHAT IS IT YOU EXPECT TO HEAR?

THAT EVERYTHING I WAS TAUGHT TO BELIEVE ISN'T FRAUD?

YOU NEED TO HAVE FAITH THAT ALL THINGS HAPPEN FOR A REASON...

...EVEN WHEN THE PURPOSE IS UNKNOWABLE.

NOT.
GOOD.
ENOUGH.

HEY...

HOW DID YOU KNOW I'D BE **HERE?**

I FIGURED YOU WANTED TO BE **ALONE...**

AND THIS, WITH GOOD REASON, IS A PLACE NO ONE DARES GO.

PLEASE, HENNI-- FOR ONCE, SHUT YOUR MOUTH AND OBEY. OUR FAMILY IS AT STAKE.
SMART GIRL.
FORGET ABOUT THE PIE. THE PIE IS NOTHING.

BUT WHAT IF IT'S EVERYTHING?

IF I'M TO COMMIT MYSELF FOR LIFE, I HAVE TO KNOW.

NO!

IF ANYTHING YOU SHOULD TRY TO UN-KNOW.

I WISH I HADN'T EVEN HEARD YOU SLANDER THE TEMPLE.

HEY LOOKOUT!
YOU'RE CROSSING THE FIRST RING!

COME BACK! YOUR SOUL IS BEING DESTROYED!

AND YET, I DON'T FEEL ANY DIFFERENT.

OKAY!
POINT MADE!
YOU'RE THE
BRAVEST EVER!

JUST DON'T
CROSS THE
RING OF DEATH!

STOP!

STOP!STOP!
STOP!STOP!
STOP!!

HENNI NO!
HELP, SOMEBODY
HELP!

I SHOULDN'T...

PRAISE HE WHO STAYED YOUR FOOT

HILDE...

...WHY WOULD GOD CREATE **FORBIDDEN LANDS?**

WHY ARE WE THE **ONLY** CREATURES WHO CAN'T SURVIVE A **CROSSING?**

AND SINCE WE "CAN'T," WHO CARVED THE TERROR HEADS?

THOSE ARE SILLY QUESTIONS.

LET'S GO HOME. YOU HAVE TO PREPARE FOR THE WEDDING FESTIVAL.
DO I?

OF COURSE.
THERE'S NOTHING ELSE YOU CAN DO!

I KNEW IT!

THE LINES ARE COMPLETELY ARBITRARY!

CONCRETE PROOF THAT WE'VE BEEN HELD IN PLACE BY NOTHING MORE THAN IRRATIONAL FEAR!
SOB

WE HAVE TO TELL EVERYONE.

STAY BACK PHANTOM!
I'M NOT DEAD.

HEY!
WHERE ARE YOU GOING?

JUST LOOK AT ME!

WE'VE
BEEN
LIED TO.

OUCH!

STOP HILDE!
NO!

HAVE YOU GONE MAD, GIRL?

SH-SHE CROSSED THE LINE OF DEATH--!
HAS SHE? HOW REMARKABLE!

IT'S A DEMON WEARING HENNI'S SKIN!!

YOU DID WELL, HILDE...

...NOW GO FETCH A STONING PARTY.

GASP

ON YOUR FEET.
COUGH
COUGH
COUGH

IT'S GETTING DARK, AND WE HAVEN'T MUCH TIME.

LOOK CLOSELY AT MY RING.

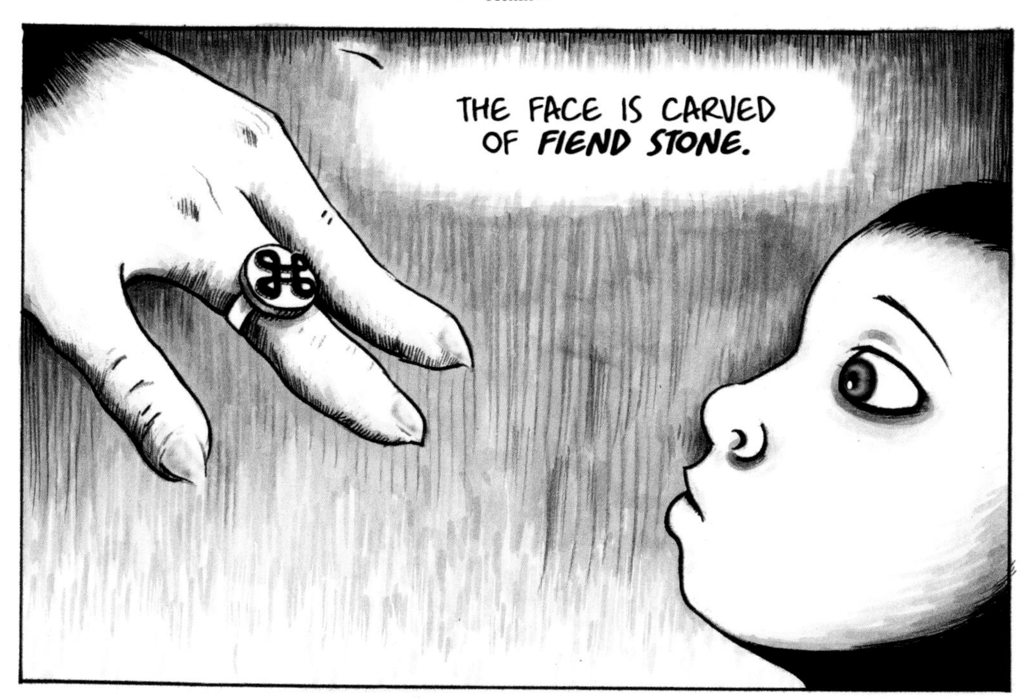
THE FACE IS CARVED OF FIEND STONE.

ARE YOU GOING TO KILL ME?

CLOSE YOUR MOUTH AND LISTEN!

DO YOU KNOW WHY THE PHOENIX FLY GLOWS?

SO WE MAY SEE ON MOONLESS NIGHTS, PERHAPS?
NO.

THEIR BLOOD IS AN UNSTABLE LUMINESCENT. PERFECTLY HARMLESS ON IT'S OWN. HOWEVER--
CRUNCH

FSSSSSHHHH

SIZZLE

IT BURNS!

WHAT DARK SORCERY IS THIS?

CHEMISTRY, ACTUALLY.

NOW GO.
BEFORE THE OTHERS RETURN.

HA HA
HA
HA
HA
HA
HA
HA!

HOLY CROW WHAT ARE THE ODDS?!

I NEVER DARED APPROACH HER BEFORE...

...HENNI'S MOTHER BEING A KNOWN FANATICAL SUPPORTER OF THE TEMPLE.

FAREWELL, DAUGHTER OF HEDRIK. MAY THE IMPROBABLE PIECE OF LUCK, THAT ALLOWED ME TO BE PRESENT FOR THIS MOMENT, BEAR OUT.

MAY WE MEET AGAIN IN THE LAND OF TRUTH AND JUSTICE...

...WHERE ALL THINGS ARE AS THEY SHOULD BE.

EVEN THOUGH I'VE DROPPED MY **ROOT VEGETABLES...**

...AND THE STENCH OF **BURNT FLESH** LINGERS ABOUT...

...WHAT A MAGNIFICENT DAY!

AH, THE MURDEROUS IMBECILES APPROACH.

...THEN THE UNGODLY CREATURE IMMOBILIZED ME WITH A DEMONIC HOWL...

...AND SHE VANISHED INTO THE DARKNESS.

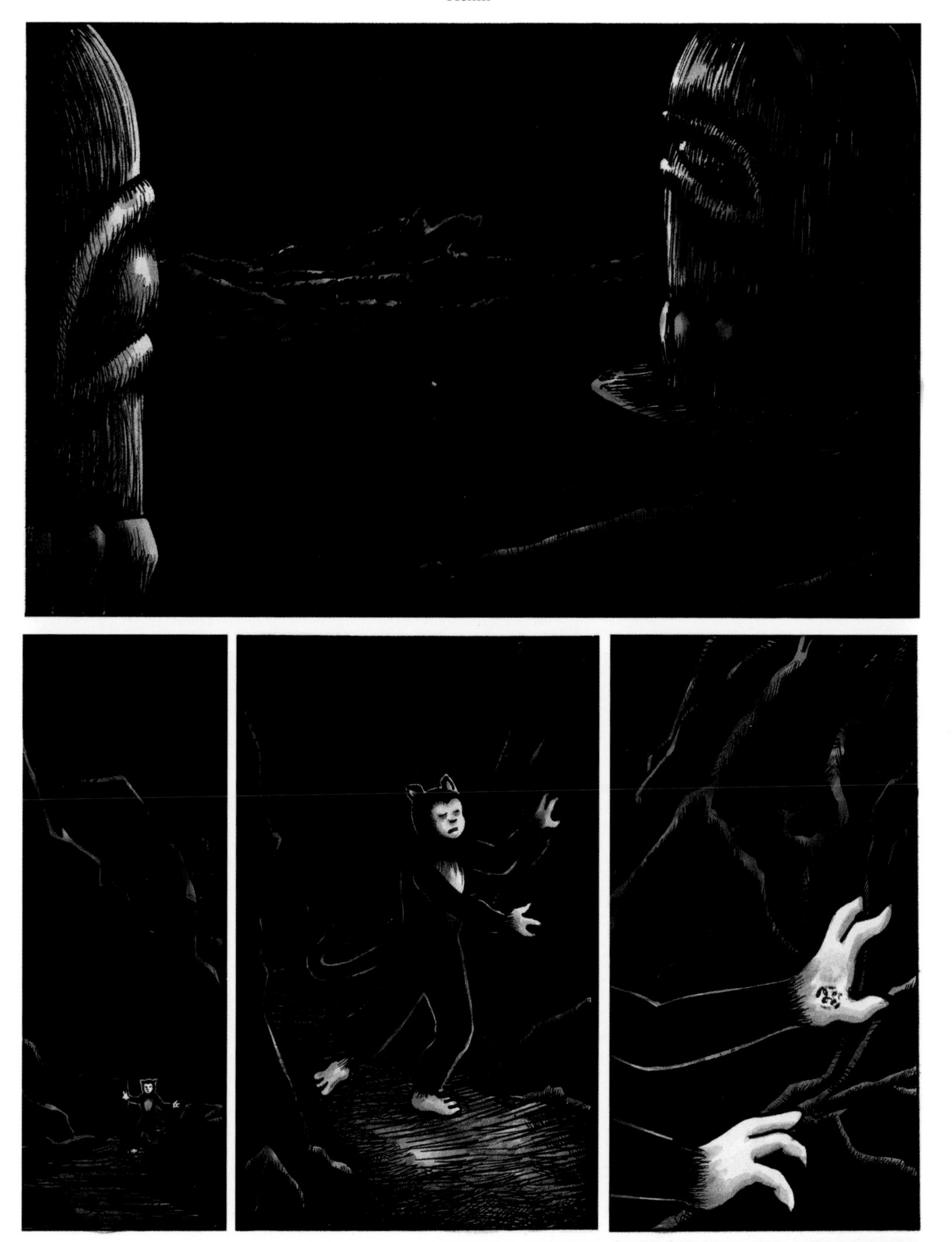

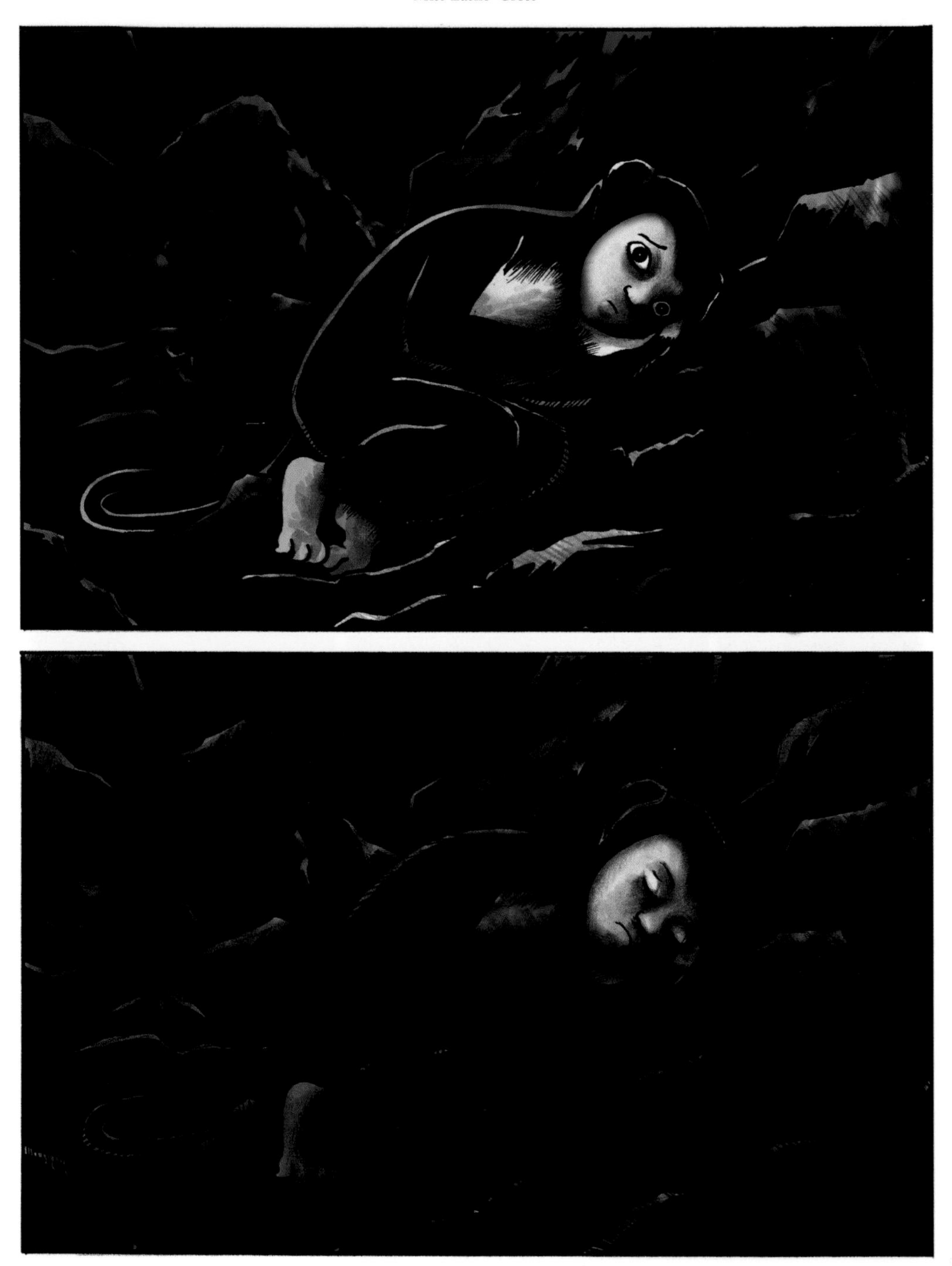

OUCH!

OUCH!
OUCH
OUCH!
OUCH!

W-WHO'S THERE?!

W-WHO'S THERE?
W-WHO'S THERE?
W-WHO'S THERE?
W- WHO'S THERE?

PLEASE, STRANGER, I NEED FOOD AND WATER!
PLEASE STRANGER, I NEED FOOD AND WATER
PLEASE STRANGER, I NEED

ONLY A DEMON COULD PERFORM SUCH MIMICRY.

WHICH PROVES THIS TO BE HELL.

FORGIVE ME...

...QUESTIONING THE DIVINE AUTHORITY OF YOUR TEMPLEMEN WAS WRONG.

THIS IS WRONG, MOTHER.
HILDE!

I'M TOO YOUNG FOR MARRIAGE, BY MANY SEASONS.

THE EXTRA GROOM WAS FATED FOR HENNI...
YOUR SISTER IS DEAD...

... BE GRATEFUL THE TEMPLEMEN RECIEVED LAST MINUTE REVELATION.

THAT I ALONE WAS "DESTINED" TO BE WED IN A FORBIDDEN MANNER?

PRAISE THE PERFECTION OF HIS PLANS!
NOW COVER YOURSELF AND JOIN THE OTHERS.

SISTER FORGIVE ME.

SLURP

ROAR!

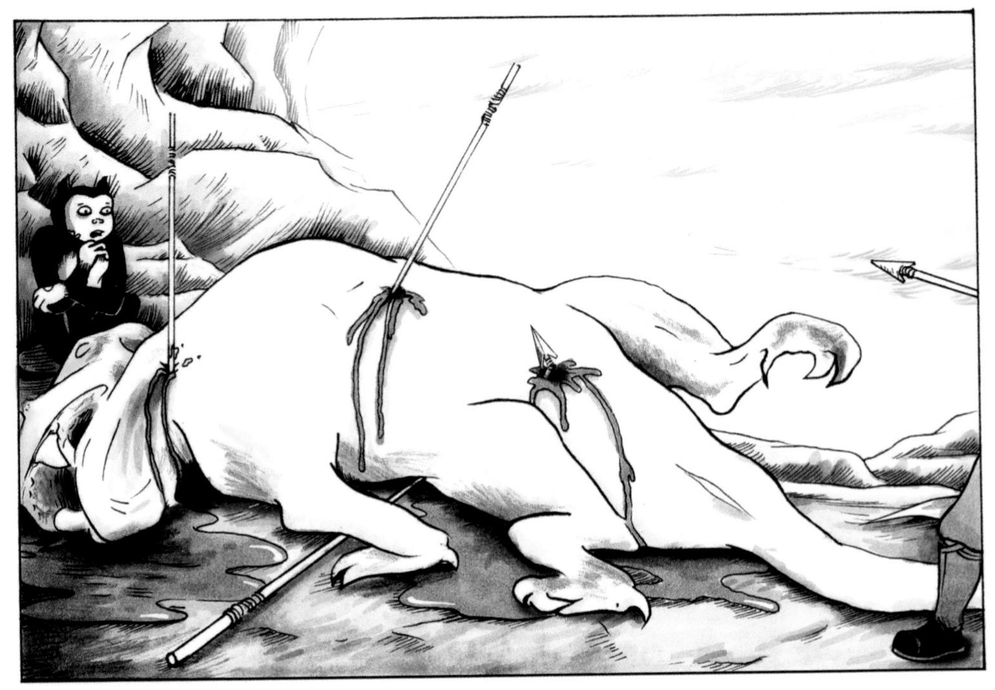

CAPTAIN! A NAKED FEMALE HAS SPRUNG FORTH FROM THE CARCASS.

IS IT A MALEVOLENT ANIMAL SPIRIT MADE FLESH...
...OR A SAVAGE?

SAVAGE!

GO HELP HIM RETRIEVE THE MEAT AND THE SAVAGE.
YES, CAPTAIN.

YOUR MEN SAVED MY LIFE.

WHAT A PRETTY LITTLE THING YOU ARE.

SHE CAN PROBABLY BE TRAINED. LET'S KEEP HER!

YOU'LL FOLLOW US TO YOUR NEW HOME.
UH, WHAT?

PREPARE TO ENTER
CIVILIZATION!

REJOICE!
THIS IS THE GREATEST DAY OF YOUR LIFE!

NAKED!
SHAMELESS!

THIS IS NOTHING LIKE MY VILLIAGE,
WE HAVE POINTED ROOFS.

ELDER HIGGEON?
KNOCK

I PRESENT A SAVAGE WENCH FROM THE NORTHERN LANDS.
PLEASED TO MEET YOU BUT...

I DON'T ACTUALLY CONSIDER MYSELF A SAVAGE.
WHILE NOT FORMALLY EDUCATED, I'M GENERALLY THOUGHT OF AS PRETTY BRIGHT.

A BARBARIAN WITH DELUSIONS OF GRANDEUR!
HA! HA! HA!

SUCH A TREAT! TO MOLD AN EMPTY ANIMAL, SUCH AS HER, INTO SOMETHING OF VALUE.

COVER THE NAKEDNESS AND PUT HER IN THE STUDY.
A CHOICE FIND CAPTAIN.

DIFFICULT TO KNOW WHERE ONE SHOULD BEGIN...
HMMMN

OKAY, "BRIGHT GIRL," TELL ME WHAT YOU "KNOW" OF CREATION.

I'VE BEEN TOLD THAT, BEFORE TIME, WHEN GOD WAS SITTING IN HIS GARDEN...
A SHARP PEBBLE CUT HIS LEG...

THE FALLEN FLESH BECAME THE EARTH...
...HIS TEARS, THE WATER...
...AND THE BLOOD FORMED THE FIRST OF MY PEOPLE.

WHAT CHILDISH NONSENSE!
THE TRUTH IS...

...GOD LIVED IN THE MEADOW OF PERFECTION, WHICH HE BUILT TO CONTAIN--
--TWO OF EVERY ANIMAL...

SEEING HOW HAPPY THEY WERE,
HE DECIDED TO MAKE A MATE FOR HIMSELF.
SO HE CREATED...

...ASHINGA WHO WAS BEAUTIFUL AND KIND...

...AND FROM HER HE MADE BEBETHE THE CLEVER HIS SECOND WIFE...

...AND FROM HER WAS BORN **ZAMERI THE OBEDIENT,**
HIS THIRD WIFE.

BEBETHE JEALOUSLY WANTED A HUSBAND FOR HERSELF ALONE. SO SHE PLOTTED WITH **SEFFER (GOD'S BROTHER)** TO--
WAIT!

"GOD'S **BROTHER?"**
DON'T INTERRUPT!

BEBETHE TOLD **ZAMERI** TO JUMP INTO THE **BOTTOMLESS WELL.**

THEN, FAKING TEARS CONVINCED ASHINGA TO HELP RETRIEVE THE **BODY**, BUT INSTEAD FELL UPON HER WITH A **BLADE**.

GOD, HAVING SEEN THIS, BANISHED HER **FOREVER**.

NOW. WHAT DOES THIS STORY **TEACH** US?

UH... CLEVERNESS LEADS TO **DAMNATION** BUT BLIND OBEDIENCE AND KINDNESS CAN GET YOU **KILLED?**
NO!

UM...GOD GAVE US FREE WILL BUT STILL EXPECTS US TO DO ONLY WHAT HE WANTS?
NO!

MORE THAN ONE WIFE IS BAD?
CERTAINLY NOT!

SIGH
THE OBVIOUS LESSON IS THAT ALL FEMALES ARE BEBETHE'S WICKED DESCENDANTS.

IT IS THE BURDEN OF MEN TO GUIDE AND RULE THEM JUSTLY.

SO YOUR EDUCATION IS MY MORAL DUTY--
KNOCK KNOCK
ELDER HIGGEON!

P-PARDON THE INTERRUPTION BUT IT'S HAPPENED AGAIN.
OUTSIDE THE NORTH GATE.

IT WAS REMOVED AND BURIED, BUT NOT BEFORE LOTS OF FOLKS SAW.

THE DISRUPTIVE ONE MUST BE STOPPED.

WHO'S THE DISRUPTOR? WHAT GOT BURIED?
SILENCE CHILD!

BUT I JUST WANT TO UNDERSTAND.

YOU D-DARE QUESTION?!

LEAVE HER BE, SHE KNOWS NO BETTER.

HENNI,
TRY TO FOCUS ONLY UPON WHAT'S RELEVANT TO YOUR STATION.

SO, IF AN **ELDER** AND A **FARMER** HAVE A **DISAGREEMENT...**
God
Clergy
Elder
Merchant
farmer
toiler

...THE **ELDER** IS IN THE **RIGHT.** NOW...
farmer
toiler

...BETWEEN A **MERCHANT** AND A **TOILER,** WHO SHOULD PREVAIL?

I **SUPPOSE** IT DEPENDS ON WHO'S IN THE **WRONG...**

HENNI, IF YOU DON'T STOP TRYING TO "UNDERSTAND" YOU CAN'T BE FILLED WITH KNOWLEDGE.

I SHOULD NEVER
HAVE COME HERE.

AHHHHH!

ZZZ

ZZZZ
WHERE DO YOU THINK YOU'RE GOING?

OUT FOR A WALK.
ELDER HIGGEON SAID NOTHING OF A WALK...

...AND WITHOUT HIS ORDERS, NOTHING IS DONE.

SO I CAN'T LEAVE?
NO.

BUT IF HE ORDERED YOU TO EAT YOUR HAT...
...THAT WOULD BE FINE?

HE WANTS ME TO EAT MY HAT?
REALLY?

UH, ACTUALLY HE SAID TO WEAR IT BACKWARDS...

OBSCENE! SACRILEGIOUS!

MOVE ALONG, GOOD PEOPLE. DO NOT LOOK!

SO BEAUTIFUL...

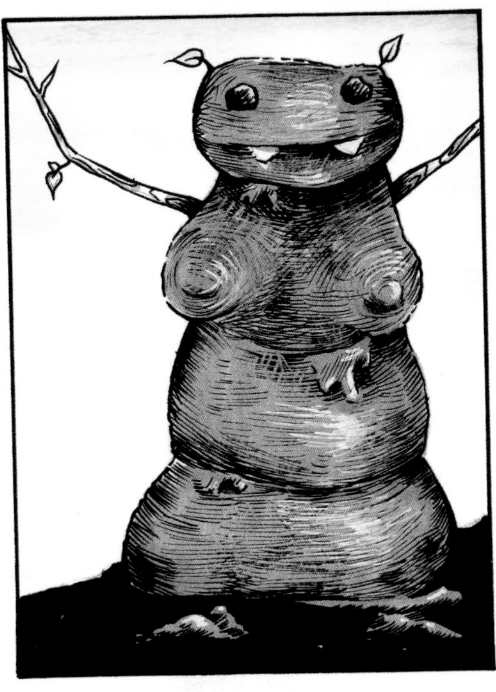

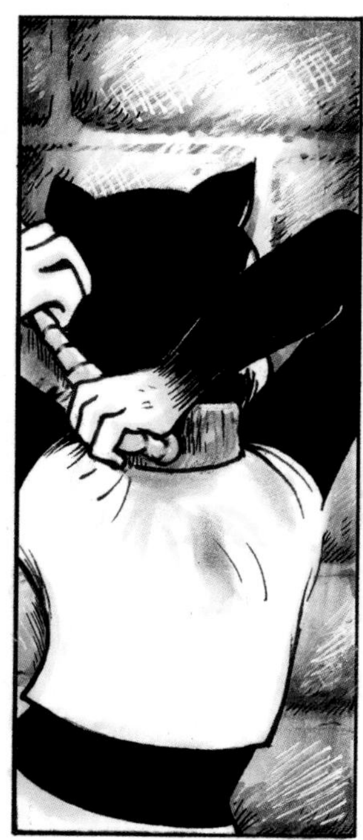

THAT WONT WORK, DEAR. OUR SHACKLES AND BOLTS ARE SOLID BOXWOOD WITH TRIPLE WOVEN LEATHER CORDS.

WE MUST BE GOOD AND WAIT.

THEY'LL REMOVE THE COLLARS AT OUR SENTENCING.

DID BOTH OF YOU ALSO LOOK UPON THE ART OF THE DISRUPTOR?

NO. MY IMPRISONMENT IS A MERE FORMALITY...
...FOR KILLING A BUSINESS RIVAL IN A DUEL.

SHE, HOWEVER, IS TO BE EXECUTED, FOR ATTEMPTED MURDER.

IT WAS AN ACCIDENT, SO HOPEFULLY THEY'LL ONLY CUT OFF MY ARM.

I KNOW I COULD LEARN TO LIVE WITH JUST ONE.

HOW CAN YOU ACCIDENTALLY TRY TO KILL SOMEONE?
WELL...

...IT HAPPENED IN A SHOP I'VE BEEN TO MANY TIMES...

...BUT NEVER BEFORE ALONE.

THE MERCHANT BEGAN SPEAKING CRUDE WORDS...

...SO I TRIED TO LEAVE.

I SHOULD HAVE RESPECTFULLY ACQUIESCED, BUT SOMEHOW...

...SOME STRANGE INSTINCT TOOK HOLD OF ME.

I PRAY THAT WHEN I'M TO BE PUNISHED...

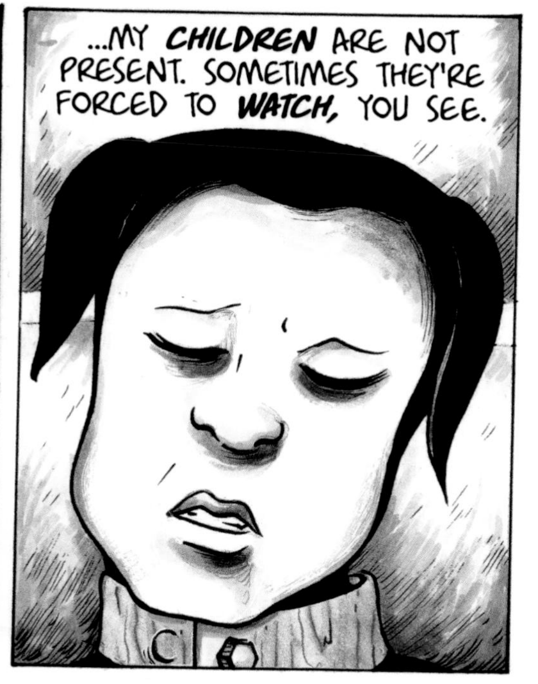
...MY CHILDREN ARE NOT PRESENT. SOMETIMES THEY'RE FORCED TO WATCH, YOU SEE.

PRISONERS! RISE FOR JUDGEMENT.

I DON'T SEE WHY I CAN'T GO FIRST.

I HAD A CLINK BALL COURSE RESERVED FOR TODAY, YOU KNOW.

YOU'RE LOOKING FOR SYMPATHY?

I'M SURE THEY WON'T REALLY KILL HER.
AFTER ALL, PEOPLE ARE GENERALLY GOOD AND REASONABLE.

I SHOULD DO SOMETHING TO HELP...

AWAHHHHHAHH
...BUT SPEAKING OUT COULD GET ME HURT TOO.

AHHHHHHH
I SHOULD MIND MY OWN BUSINESS AND RESPECT THEIR WAYS.

GO SAVAGE, MEET YOUR FATE.

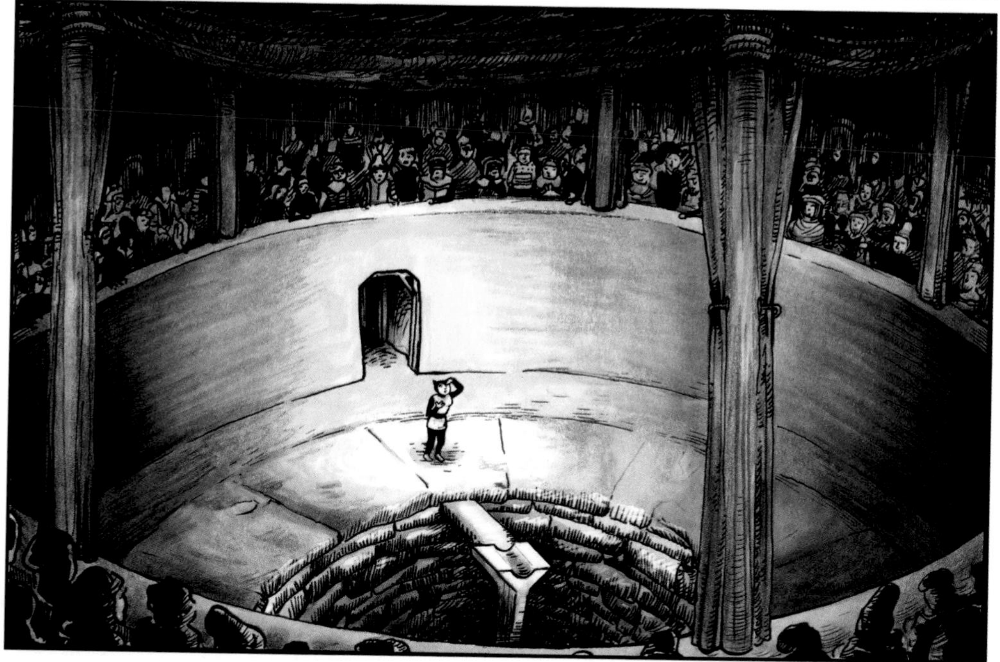

BRING BACK MY MAMA!

MAMA!

HENNI HOGARTHE,

CHARGED WITH FLAGRANT CONNOISSEURSHIP OF BLASPHEMOUS ARTS.

ELDER HIGGEON, HOW DOES SHE PLEAD?
GUILTY!

WHAT?

AND, LET IT BE PUBLICLY KNOWN, SHE ACTED WITH NEITHER MY KNOWLEDGE...

...NOR CONSENT! AN ABUSE OF MY TRUST...

......AND THE HONOR OF MY HOUSE!

DULY NOTED, ELDER. THE ACCUSED IS FOUND GUILTY.

AS IT IS A FIRST OFFENSE, SHE SHALL HAVE ONLY ONE EYE PUT OUT, TO DISCOURAGE FURTHER ENJOYMENT OF THE VISUAL ARTS...

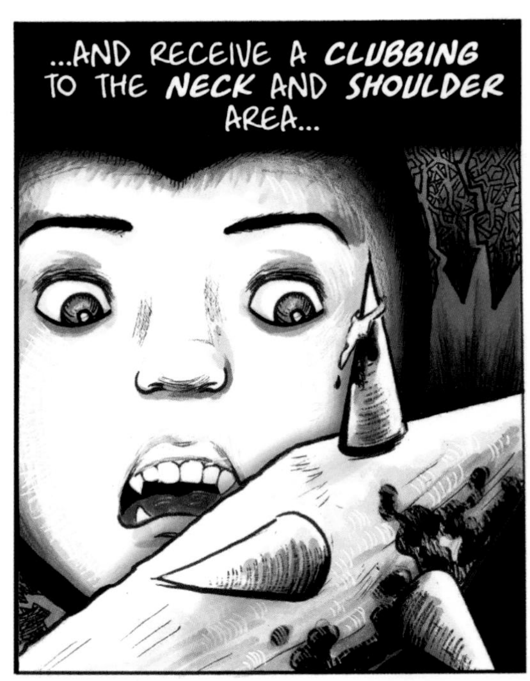
...AND RECEIVE A CLUBBING TO THE NECK AND SHOULDER AREA...

OF NOT MORE THAN-

MUCH GRATITUDE SIR!

HOW'S THAT?

FOR THROUGH YOUR JUDGEMENT, YOU SEEM TO ESTABLISH BARBARIANS AS THE EQUALS OF YOUR PEOPLE.

GASP!

THE MUTILATION OF MY BODY WILL SEND A MESSAGE OF BROTHERHOOD AND EQUALITY TO THOSE WHO PREVIOUSLY CONSIDERED THEMSELVES BENEATH SUCH HIGH MORAL STANDARDS.

FOR, THEY'LL UNDERSTAND A FEW DAYS TRAINING IS SUFFICIENT TO JOIN YOUR NOBLE RACE.

TO SUGGEST SO IS SCANDALOUS....
WRONG!
NEVER!
OBSCENE!

YES. I DO FEEL UNWORTHY OF THIS RADICALLY PROGRESSIVE JUDGE...

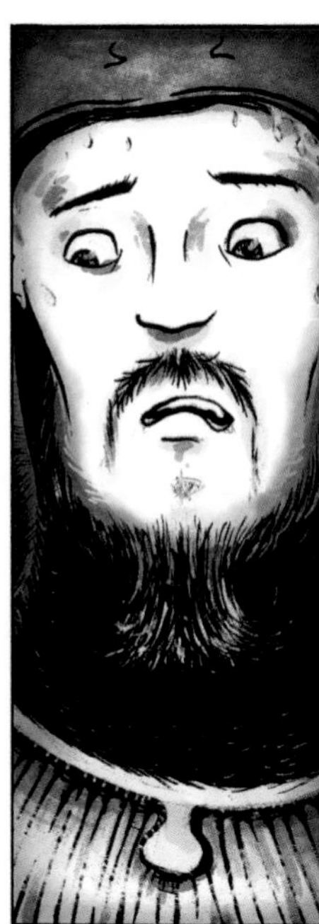

...AND HIS BOLD STEP TOWARDS A TOLERANT MULTI-CULTURAL UTOPIA.

JUST IMAGINE,
NUDITY
INTERFAITH LOVE
GOVERNMENT CULTURAL EXCHANGE
MIXED MARRIAGE!

PERHAPS MERE BANISHMENT WILL DO?
YOU EXPECT TO GO UNPUNISHED?

SIR, TO HAVE BRIEFLY KNOWN THE COMPANY OF PEOPLES SO SMART, WELL MANNERED...

...AND FINELY DRESSED AS YOURSELVES...

...ONLY TO BE EXILED?

THE COMMONERS ARE EATING THIS UP, KILL HER NOW!
I DARE NOT, IF IT APPEARS TO DIMINISH US.

FEIGN DISINTEREST AND RELEASE HER FOR NOW.
THE DISGRACE!

BANISHMENT IS EXACTLY WHAT YOU SHALL SUFFER!

WHAT A WICKED THING I'VE BECOME.

DISHONORABLE
BUT FREE.

I'LL BEGIN DISPERSING MY ASSASSINS, IN CIVILIAN GARB, TO EVERY NEIGHBORING VILLAGE.

NO MATTER WHERE SHE MAY CHOSE TO ATTACK NEXT, THEY'LL CONTEND WITH NOTHING MORE NOTABLE THAN A MURDERED VAGRANT

I SHOULD LEAVE A MARK SO I DON'T GET LOST.

H

SO DARK...

OH!

NOW THAT'S WEIRD.

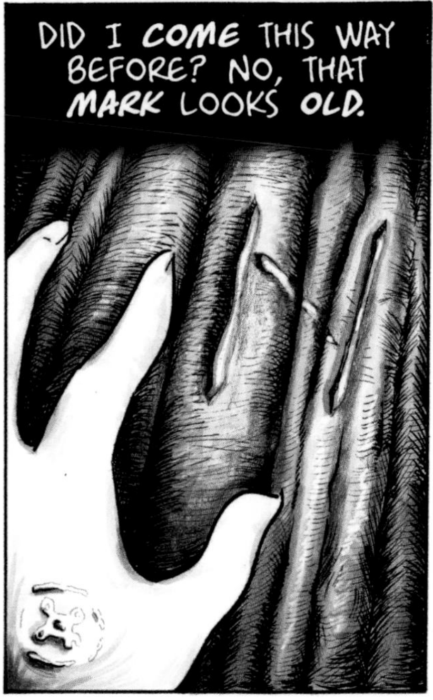
DID I COME THIS WAY BEFORE? NO, THAT MARK LOOKS OLD.

COME IN.
FOLLOW
MY VOICE.

THAT ACCENT...
YOU'RE FROM
THE NORTH?

YES?

YES.
BUMP
EXCUSE ME.
COLD CLAY?
A SCULPTURE.
OH!
YOU'RE THE DISRUPTOR!

HA!

IS THAT WHAT THEY CALL ME?

WELL THEN, WELCOME TO THE DISRUPTOR'S LAIR.

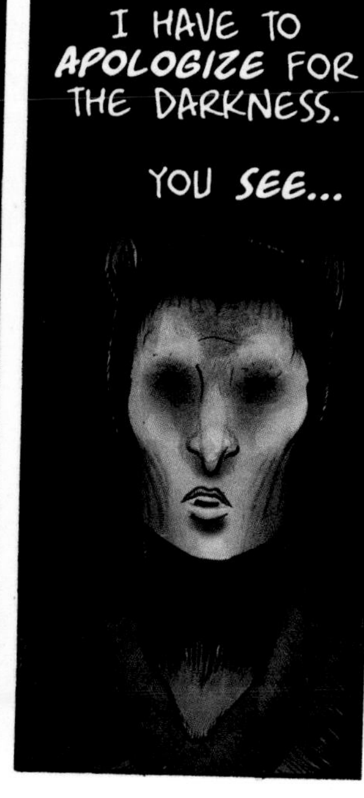
I HAVE TO APOLOGIZE FOR THE DARKNESS.
YOU SEE...

IT MAKES NO DIFFERENCE TO ME.

OH! WHERE ARE YOUR EYES?

THEY'RE OFF VISITING FRIENDS.

BUT HOW?
NO, DEAR.

I SUPPOSE YOU'RE UNACCUSTOMED TO SARCASM.
I'VE READ OF ITS USAGE.

THEY WERE CUT FROM MY HEAD MANY YEARS AGO.

HOW TERRIBLE. I'M SORRY.

HAVE A SEAT, I'LL TELL YOU WHAT HAPPENED.

MY FATHER WAS A GREAT COURT PAINTER, TRAINING ME TO FOLLOW IN HIS FOOTSTEPS.

BE SURE TO CAPTURE MY REGAL BEAUTY.

BUT AFTER THE REVOLUTION...

WHAT KIND OF REVOLUTION?

THE USUAL KIND--
--BEST INTENTIONS, POWER VACUUM, COUP, MISERY.

ANYWAY, ALL SECULAR ART WAS BANNED.

AT FIRST FATHER WAS BRAVE.

DEFIANT.

BUT HE HAD MOTHER AND I TO THINK OF...

...SO HE SIGNED A "CONFESSION" AND SPENT THE REST OF HIS LIFE AS A SCRIBE...

...ENDLESSLY **COPYING** THE HOLY TEXTS.

NO! NO, SCRIBE.

TOO MUCH **COLOR.**

THE HANDWRITING IS MUCH TOO **SENSUAL.**

HE GREW BITTER...

...A DEFEATED MAN.

ON HIS DEATHBED HE TOLD ME NOT TO BE A COWARD.

DON'T LIVE ON YOUR KNEES AS I HAVE.

SO I'VE TAKEN RISKS AND PAID THE PRICE,
BUT I REGRET NOTHING.

NOW... YOU CAN SPEND THE NIGHT, IF YOU LIKE, OR PERHAPS YOU COULD HELP ME WITH SOMETHING.
WHAT?

THERE'S A SCULPTURE OUT BACK, TOO HEAVY FOR ME ALONE.

IT'S BEEN A WHILE SINCE I'VE HAD A VISIT FROM ONE OF MY SUPPORTERS, AND I'D LOVE TO INSTALL IT AT THE SOUTHERN GATE.

YOU WANT ME TO RISK GOING BACK?

I UNDERSTAND YOUR RELUCTANCE.

IT WOULD BE HARD WORK, AND I CAN'T PAY ANYTHING, BUT...

...IT WOULD BE VERY KIND OF YOU.

WELL...

YOUR WORK IS BEAUTIFUL.

AND I'D BE HONORED TO HELP.

I DON'T MEAN TO BE RUDE, BUT WHAT'S THE POINT?

YOUR WORK IS ALWAYS DESTROYED BY THE VILLAGE GUARD.

I'M WELL AWARE.

SO WHY DO YOU BRING IT THERE? TO MOCK THEM? FOR REVENGE?

ART NEEDS AN AUDIENCE.

BUT THEY HATE YOU.
EVERYONE AGREES WITH THE ELDERS.

THERE'S A DIFFERENCE BETWEEN **OBEYING** AND **AGREEING.**

GUARDS!

THEY'LL HACK IT TO PIECES.

SO IT WAS ALL FOR NOTHING.

I DON'T FEEL THAT WAY..

TAKE A CLOSER LOOK AT "EVERYONE..."

AWESOME!

I SEE WHAT YOU MEAN.

I DON'T THINK I EVER REALIZED, OBEYING IS NOT THE SAME AS AGREEING.

NOW... THERE'S ANOTHER VILLAGE, VERY SIMILAR TO THIS ONE, I'M AFRAID...

..ABOUT A DAY'S WALK DOWN THE ROAD.

THANKS FOR ALL YOUR HELP.
IT WAS MY PLEASURE.

I KNOW THAT MARK!

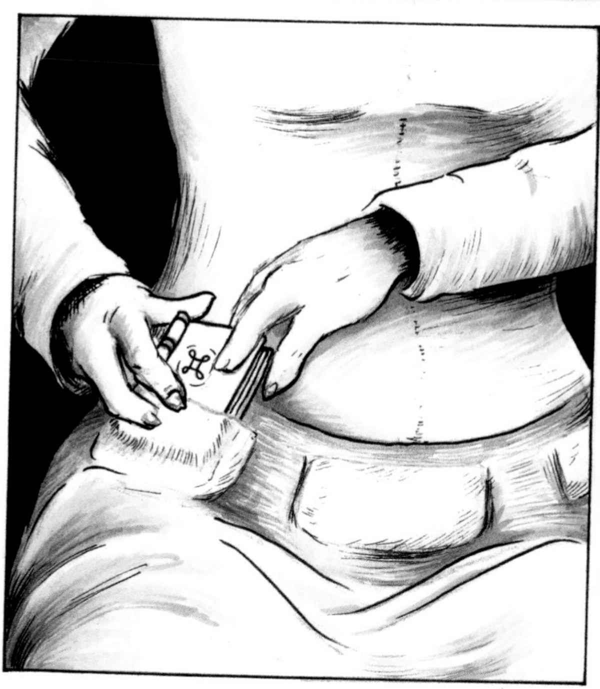

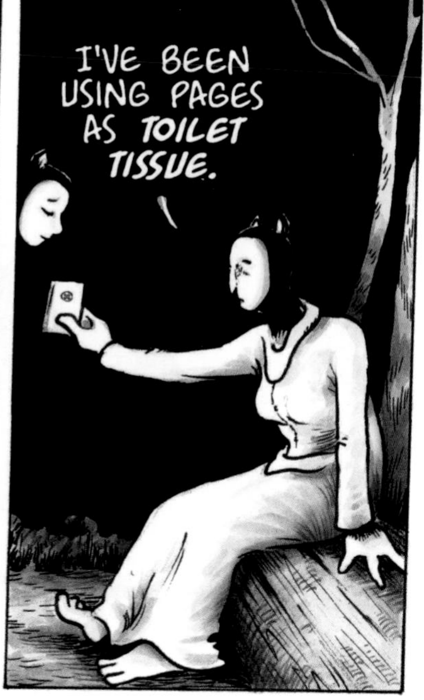
I'VE BEEN USING PAGES AS TOILET TISSUE.

THIS WAS MY FATHER'S!
WHERE DID YOU FIND IT?!
Hedrik Hogarthe

AMONG A PILE OF ROBES, BY EARTHEND FALLS, JUST OVER THAT HILL.

THANKS AGAIN!

IS IT POSSIBLE DAD IS ONLY "DEAD" AS I AM CONSIDERED "DEAD" BY OUR PEOPLE?

I WILL FIND HIM.

SOMEHOW.

BUT...
THAT'S JUST IMPOSSIBLE.

NO ONE COULD--
--I CAN'T CLIMB THAT.

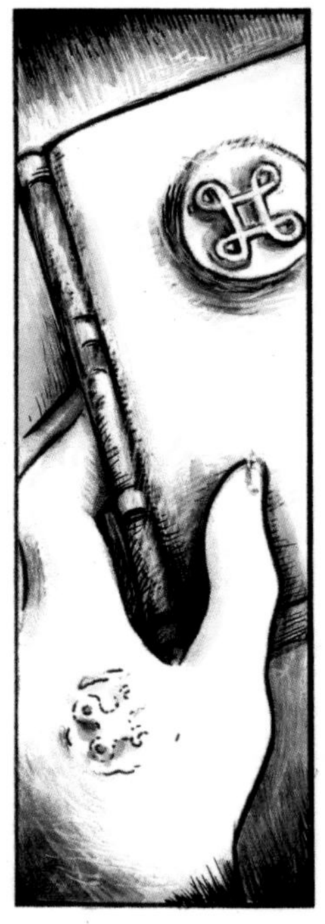

HMMMN... NOT A LOT OF PAGES LEFT... PAPER SMELLS MOLDY. SOMETHING STUCK...

...TO THE PAGE BACK.

A MAP...
The Thestlan board of Tourism presents:
wonders of civilization
The Great Public Library: (homre of the world famous Singing Librarians!)
1
Colossus of the
2
3

...WITH NOTES.
DEAREST H,
THIS DREADFUL "MAP" PREDATES THE CRUSADES AND GREAT CONQUEST, HOWEVER, I'VE ADDED SOME PERTINENT INFORMATION, GAINED AT GREAT COST BY OUR CONTACTS. MEMORIZE AS BEST YOU CAN, THEN DISCARD (FOR OBVIOUS REASONS). GOOD LUCK, FRIEND, MAY WE MEET AGAIN IN THE LAND OF TRUTH AND JUSTICE WHERE EVERYTHING IS AS IT SHOULD BE. TILL THEN,
-B-

NO ONE CAN KNOW THE CONTENTS OF ANOTHER'S MIND...

BUT, IF I WANTED TO LIVE A LIE, I WOULD'VE NEVER LEFT MY HOME.

SOMEWHERE, A LAND OF "TRUTH...

...AND JUSTICE" EXISTS.

WHERE JUST BEING ME...

...WOULD BE ENOUGH.

MORE IMPORTANTLY, DAD MAY BE THERE.
ALIVE!

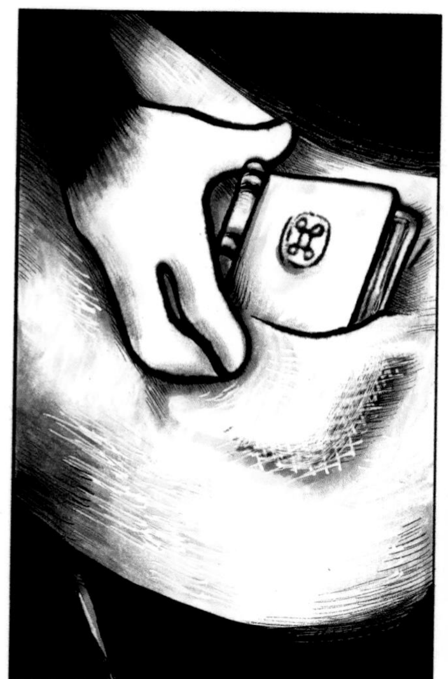

Acknowledgments:

Special thanks to Kevin Colden, Bobby Timony, Tracey and Jon S., Karen Green, Phil Jackson, and everyone at House Of Twelve